PARTNERS·FOR·LIFE

PARTNERS·FOR·LIFE

The Mysteries of Animal Symbiosis

BY MARGERY FACKLAM

ILLUSTRATIONS BY PAMELA JOHNSON

SIERRA CLUB BOOKS
San Francisco

LITTLE, BROWN AND COMPANY
Boston • Toronto • London

The Sierra Club, founded in 1892 by John Muir, has devoted itself to the study and protection of the earth's scenic and ecological resources—mountains, wetlands, woodlands, wild shores and rivers, deserts and plains. The publishing program of the Sierra Club offers books to the public as a nonprofit educational service in the hope that they may enlarge the public's understanding of the Club's basic concerns. The Sierra Club has some sixty chapters in the United States and in Canada. For information about how you may participate in its programs to preserve wilderness and the quality of life, please address inquiries to Sierra Club, 730 Polk Street, San Francisco, CA 94109.

A LUCAS • EVANS BOOK

Text copyright © 1989 by Margery Facklam

Illustrations copyright © 1989 by Pamela Johnson

First edition

Sierra Club Books/Little, Brown children's books
are published by Little, Brown and Company (Inc.) in association with Sierra Club Books.
Published simultaneously in Canada by Little, Brown & Company (Canada) Limited

Printed in the United States of America

Library of Congress Cataloging-in-Publication Data

Facklam, Margery.
  Partners for life.
  "A Lucas-Evans book"
  Includes index.
  Summary: Examines partnerships between two different species of animals that provide one or both of the partners with food, protection, transportation, or a way to keep clean.
  1. Symbiosis—Juvenile literature.   2. Animal behavior—Juvenile literature.   3. Animal ecology—Juvenile literature. [1. Symbiosis.   2. Animals—Habits and behavior] I. Johnson, Pamela, ill.   II. Title.
QH548.F28 1989   591.5'2482   88-35929
ISBN 0-316-25983-7
10 9 8 7 6 5 4 3 2 1

CONTENTS

1   TEAMWORK   7

2   INSECT PARTNERS   11

3   PARTNERS IN THE SEA   15

4   BIRD PARTNERS   24

5   MICROSCOPIC PARTNERS   29

6   PARASITE PARTNERS   35

7   NATURE'S BALANCING ACT   41

INDEX   46

1
TEAMWORK

When a Nile crocodile opens its huge mouth and lets a bird walk right in to poke around for scraps of food, it's not because the two animals are friends. It's strictly business.

There are many such partnerships between species. Some animals team up with other species that help them find food or that give them shelter or protection; others have partners that keep them clean and tidy. Some animals change

partners after a brief visit; others stick together for a lifetime, and in these partnerships, one or sometimes both of the animals could not survive without the other. Many partnerships are between two individual animals, and others are between groups of animals.

Such teamwork between two different species is called *symbiosis* (sim-bee-OH-sis), and there are three different kinds: mutualism, commensalism, and parasitism.

Mutualism (MEW-choo-al-is-um) is a partnership that helps both animals. An example of a mutual partnership is the team of the crocodile and the bird that walks right into its mouth. While the bird finds food the crocodile gets its teeth cleaned.

Commensalism (com-MEN-sal-is-um) is one-sided symbiosis. This kind of partnership helps one of the animals but neither helps nor harms the other. Commensal means "dining at the same table," with one animal as the host. At a party, the host supplies the place and the food. In a commensal team, the host may provide transportation, food, shelter, or protection. A shark, for example, is the host for remora fish that hitch rides on the shark's back and belly, where they can pick up scraps of food.

Parasitism (PAIR-a-sit-is-um) is a partnership in which one animal benefits, while the other is harmed. A parasite is like an uninvited guest who takes over the host's party and moves in, sometimes permanently. The parasite steals nourishment from its host, but it must not take too much. If the host dies, the parasite will die, too—unless it can move out and find a new place to eat. A tapeworm, for example, can live in a cat's intestine as long as the worm doesn't grow too fast and make the cat sick. If a dog infested with fleas becomes sick, the fleas jump off in search of a healthier host.

Symbiosis occurs between the largest and smallest of creatures and in all kinds of habitats, from coral reefs in the ocean to the stomachs of cows. Wherever it is found, this kind of teamwork is not a once-in-a-while part of an animal's life. It is not an accidental partnership such as we see when a dog adopts orphaned kittens or wolf cubs, for example. Symbiosis is programmed into the behavior of the whole species and is part of the life cycle of each animal.

The same three kinds of symbiosis—mutualism, commensalism, and parasitism—are also found between plants, and between plants and animals. There may be thousands of examples of symbiosis we don't yet know of or understand. This book is about some of the amazing animal partners scientists have seen and studied.

2
INSECT PARTNERS

Ants seem to be everywhere, and it's no wonder. There are more than eight thousand different species, and there are billions of each kind. Most ants have partners, but most common and easiest to watch are the ants that keep herds of aphid "cattle."

Aphids are tiny plant lice. There are hundreds of different kinds, each named for the plant it lives on—banana aphids, bamboo aphids, oak aphids, rose aphids, cabbage aphids, apple aphids, and so on. Wherever they live, aphids cause damage. They poke their hollow beaks into stems and leaves to suck sap from their host plants. While they take vital food from plants, they also spread diseases.

All aphids excrete honeydew, which is neither honey nor dew but rather left-over sugar and water from the plant sap they drink. Sometimes in bright sunlight you can see dried crystals of honeydew glistening like frost on leaves.

Gardeners try to get rid of aphids, but ants collect them. When an ant wants a drink, it taps an aphid's back with its antennae, and the aphid gives it a drop of honeydew. Some ants gather and store honeydew in their nests. In return, the ants protect the helpless aphids when bigger insects try to catch and eat them.

Another kind of ant builds sheds from bits of leaves and bark and herds its aphids into these shelters each night. In cornfields yet another kind of ant col-lects the eggs of corn aphids in autumn and stores them in underground nests, where they stay warm all winter. In spring, the ants carry the aphid eggs out of the nests and put them on the roots of new corn plants. As soon as they hatch, the young aphids begin to suck the sweet sap from the corn roots, and the ants once again have fresh honeydew to drink.

Some butterfly caterpillars also se-crete honeydew from glands on their backs, and they have ant partners who "dine at their table" as commensal part-ners. One butterfly called the "large blue" has a mutual partnership with one spe-cies of red ant. The large blue's ant part-ners thrive in heavily grazed meadows where an herb called thyme grows wild.

The butterfly female lays its eggs on the leaves of the thyme plants. After the eggs hatch, the young caterpillars eat the leaves and secrete honeydew on their backs for the red ants to drink. When the caterpillars are ready to molt for their next change, they stop eating thyme

leaves, and the ants drag them into underground nests.

Though the red ants attack any invader that tries to destroy their own newly hatched young, they allow their guest caterpillar to eat some of the tiny ant larvae. Finally the well-fed caterpillar attaches itself to the roof of the ants' burrow and spins a kind of cocoon called a chrysalis around itself for the winter. When the new large blue butterfly emerges in spring, it crawls out of the ants' nest, opens its wings, and flies away. The ants look for another large blue caterpillar.

In England, the large blue butterfly is extinct. The last one was seen there in 1979. As more houses were built and more land was plowed for crops or planted with orchards and forests, the habitats of the large blue butterflies and their ant partners simply disappeared. When scientists tried to raise the large blue butterflies without their ant partners, they found it couldn't be done.

Ants are not always such willing partners, however. When a bluejay or a robin goes "anting" to try to get rid of itchy feather mites, the ants do not volunteer their services as they do with the large blue butterfly. Birds search out mounds of formic ants, which protect themselves by squirting burning formic acid from glands in their abdomens. Grabbing an ant in its beak, a bird pushes the ant under its wing or between its feathers. The ant reacts by bombarding the bird with a tiny spray of formic acid, which kills the feather mites and other parasites.

3
PARTNERS IN THE SEA

If you could snorkel over a coral reef, you might see a fish swim to its death among the waving tentacles of an animal that looks like a plant. That animal, called a sea anemone (a-NEM-o-nee), stings the fish with poison from its tentacles and eats it. But you might also see another little fish, called the clown fish or damselfish, settle in among the tentacles of that same ane-

mone without harm. Why is one fish killed while the other is safe from the anemone's poison?

The clown fish and the anemone have an amazing partnership. Many small animals wear dull colors that blend with their background, but the clown fish is as vivid as a neon sign. Its dazzling orange body is wrapped in three bands of white outlined in black. It's easy for a big fish on the prowl for food to find a clown fish. So to protect itself, the clown fish has learned to hide in plain sight in the anemone.

An anemone is an invertebrate; it has no backbone or skeleton. Its soft body is little more than a stout hollow tube that opens at one end into a mouth surrounded by tentacles. At the other end is a slimy disk on which the anemone can slide along at the speed of a snail or hang onto wave-washed rocks with the grip of a bulldog. Anemones come in many sizes and colors. They look harmless, but they're not. The thousands of microscopic stinging cells in the anemone's tentacles are powerful weapons.

For a long time, marine biologists thought that all clown fish were immune to the poison of all anemones, but then they learned that each fish has to develop its own partnership with care.

When a clown fish chooses an anemone for its hiding place, it swims close to the tentacles, careful not to brush against them at first. After a few minutes, the little fish darts close to touch a tentacle quickly with its tail or a fin. If its scales stick to the anemone, it pulls free.

Fish have a slippery coating of mucus that protects their scales from damage and disease. Every time a stinging cell of the anemone injects the clown fish with a bit of poison, the fish's coating of mucus changes. In some way that scientists haven't quite figured out, the mucus becomes immune to the poison, perhaps in the same way we become immune to diseases when we are vaccinated against them.

Slowly the clown fish becomes bolder. It may take an hour or more of darting in and out among the tentacles before the fish is safe from the anemone's poison. But if the clown fish stays away from its friendly anemone for more than an hour, it loses the protection and must start all over again. Although several clown fish can live among the tentacles of a single anemone, they are safe only in that one anemone. If they swim into the waiting tentacles of a strange anemone, they will be stung by the poison and eaten.

In exchange for a safe hideout, the clown fish becomes bait for the anemone's dinner. Lured by this bright-orange fish that doesn't even try to get away, a bigger fish swims right into the anemone's tentacles to be stung and eaten. And like a good partner, the clown fish cleans up the leftovers when the anemone has finished eating.

A bright blue-and-silver fish called the horse mackerel has the same kind of partnership with a jellyfish known as the Portuguese man-of-war. Some people call this jellyfish a "before-the-wind-sailor" because its sky-blue bubble, crested with a pink ruffle, sails above the water. Fleets of these "sailors" glistening in the sun are beautiful to watch but dangerous to meet. A sting from a man-of-war can kill a swimmer. Under the man-of-war's gas-filled bag of "jelly," long tentacles trail below the surface of the sea. They are streamers of death to any fish that gets tangled in them. Dozens of these tentacles, some sixty feet long, wrap around the fish and sting it to death. They draw the dead fish up into the man-of-war's floating bubble, where it is digested.

But the horse mackerel can live safely among these deadly tentacles, protected from bigger fish. And like the clown fish, the little mackerel acts as bait for its partner's meals.

Not all underwater partners team up for protection; some offer other services.

Imagine how annoying it would be to have an itch you couldn't scratch. Animals without hands or feet or long swishing tails can't chase away insects or remove pesky parasites that burrow under scales or skin. Instead of grooming themselves, these fish have learned to go to the cleaners.

Sharks, barracudas, and moray eels are the tough guys of the sea. They're quick to gobble up any little fish that get too close. So most small fish stay as far away as they can from these fierce predators. How, then, do they call a truce long enough to let one another know they are ready to form a partnership?

Most cleaner fish advertise. The tiny cigar-shaped wrasse stands on its head and wiggles in a kind of dance that lets the big fish know the cleaning station is open for business. When it sees the cleaner's signal, the big "client" fish slows down or stops moving and opens its mouth wide. The big fish waits for a cleaner fish to swim inside its mouth and pick parasites and bits of food from its teeth and gills.

There's often a waiting line for a turn with a cleaner fish. Like cars lining up for a car wash, fleets of enormous manta rays cruise close to a coral reef where wrasse fish are working. The wrasse's usual customers might be three-hundred-pound groupers and other big fish around the reef, but sometimes whole schools of fish leave their migration route to stop off for cleaning. A diver at one coral reef watched a single cleaner fish called the senorita. In one hour, that senorita fish picked the parasites from more than three hundred big fish!

The blenny is a small fish without a partner, but it has found a way to protect itself by acting as a copycat. Although it's not in the cleaning business, the blenny fools the bigger fish. When it dances on its head like the wrasse, the blenny can get close to a bigger fish and nibble on its leftovers without danger of being eaten itself.

Sharks, sea turtles, and whales travel with their partners, the remoras. Their partnerships are commensal, with the small fish getting the benefit. The remora is nicknamed suckerfish, or shark sucker, because it has a suction disk on top of its head that attaches to the tail, fin, shell, or underbelly of its big partner. And it can really hang on!

On one of his journeys to the New World, Christopher Columbus watched the Indians fish for sea turtles. They'd tie a suckerfish on a line and throw it into the ocean. When the suckerfish fastened itself to a turtle, the fisherman had only to haul in the line to catch both the turtle and its remora bait.

The huge manta rays, sharks, and sea

turtles are messy eaters. They leave lots of scraps, and when they do, the remoras disconnect their suction cups to swim free and join in the feast.

A hermit is usually an animal or person who lives alone. Despite its name, the hermit crab is another sea creature that lives with a partner. But before it can team up with another animal, the hermit crab must first find a shell. Since it doesn't own one, it borrows a shell to protect its soft body. Like a person trying on clothes, the little crab backs in and crawls out of empty whelk or sea-snail shells until it finds one that fits just right.

Once settled in its new house, the hermit crab goes looking for a sea anemone or sponge willing to let go its tight hold on a rock and ride on top of the shell. The anemone gets scraps from the crab's meals; in return, it protects the crab with its stinging tentacles and camouflages the bare white borrowed shell. As the hermit crab grows and moves into larger shells, it often collects several anemones or sponges to ride along.

Most of what we know about underwater partnerships was learned from divers who watch fish in warm and shallow tropical seas. In the deeper seas or in the frigid Arctic and Antarctic oceans, where it's more difficult to dive, there may be other animal partnerships to be discovered.

4
BIRD PARTNERS

Most birds know enough to steer clear of large animals with huge mouths and big teeth, such as a twelve-foot Nile crocodile that can snap up a bird in the blink of an eye. But a long-legged African wading bird called the Egyptian plover has earned the name "crocodile bird" because it walks fearlessly into the huge reptile's mouth.

Not much bothers the tough hide of

a crocodile, but the soft tissue inside its mouth is easily infested with parasites. When the crocodile wants its teeth cleaned, it lies on the riverbank with its mouth wide open to let the plover know it's ready. The long-billed bird hops in, picks between the croc's sharp teeth, and pokes under its thick tongue, then moves on to the next crocodile customer.

Another long-legged African bird, the cattle egret, doesn't stick with one kind of partner, but moves from gazelles to zebras to antelopes to giraffes, and even to elephants. It's a small species of heron that especially likes to eat grasshoppers, which are hard to find because they are the same color as the grass. But when herd animals such as zebras and elephants stomp through the grass, grasshoppers fly up all around them, and the hungry egrets snatch the insects out of the air.

In return, the egrets provide an alarm system. When they hear a leopard or other predator, the birds screech and flap their wings to let the herds know it's time to be alert.

Egrets aren't at all fussy about who kicks up the fresh grasshoppers. They seem just as eager to follow farm plows pulled by oxen or buffalo as they do to move with wild herds. And since egrets began to appear in South America and later in North America, in the 1930s, they have also followed tractors.

An African and Asian bird called the oxpecker is more likely to stick around one partner. With sharp claws and a long stiff tail for balance, an oxpecker hangs onto a large animal the way a woodpecker hangs onto a tree. It sets up housekeeping on a buffalo or warthog, using its long curved bill to dig out ticks that have burrowed into its partner's hide. The oxpecker thrives not on the tick but on the blood the tick has taken from the mammal.

The oxpecker also flaps and flutters and screeches in alarm to let its host know that danger is near, but it doesn't stop at that. If the buffalo seems to pay no attention to the alarm, the oxpecker raps the big beast on the head with its beak until the animal moves.

The cowbird is another cleaning partner to large grazing animals. A hundred or so years ago, cowbirds followed the huge herds of bison that thundered across the plains of America. They ate insects and parasites from the bisons' thick coats.

Because they were always on the move, cowbirds didn't have time to build nests and settle down long enough to hatch eggs. They began to lay eggs in other birds' nests and leave the hatching to the foster mother.

Right now scientists are watching cowbirds with great interest to see how they are adapting to changing conditions. Without bison herds to follow, cowbirds have adjusted to a more settled life among herds of cattle on ranches. Now that they more often stay in one place, will they begin to build their own nests?

A small African bird called the honey guide has a strange partnership with a tough little member of the weasel family called the honey badger. Despite the sweet name, honey badgers are feisty, powerful animals built low to the ground on short, thick legs. Their teeth are so strong that they can bite through a tortoise shell. Their skin is so thick and firm that it's not easily pierced by a snakebite or a bee sting. A honey badger, whose other name is ratel, will eat almost anything, including birds, eggs, reptiles, amphibians, and insects. But what it really loves is honey.

The honey guide is the perfect partner for the badger. It searches out bees' nests, but not for the honey. It wants only to eat the wax and bee grubs. However, the small bird can't break open the bee's nest, which is usually secure inside a tree trunk. So when the honey guide sees a honey badger, it flits and flutters around and screeches until it has the badger's attention; then it leads the badger to the

nest. The badger scrambles up the tree and quickly rips open the bees' nest with its long front claws, paying no attention to the angry bees.

People who love honey have learned that if they follow a honey guide, they can often beat the honey badger to the bees' nest. The bird doesn't seem to care whom it teams up with so long as it gets the juicy bee grubs and wax.

Some symbiotic relationships involve more than just two individual partners. When whole groups of animals team up, scientists call it *social symbiosis*. Some flocks of birds, for example, fly together for safety. Slate-colored juncos and chipping sparrows feed on the ground, but they travel with chickadees and warblers that feed higher in the trees. Because the ground birds are easy prey to cats and other predators, they rely on the birds feeding in the trees to be their early-warning system. When a chickadee or warbler calls an alarm, the ground birds take to the air.

5
MICROSCOPIC PARTNERS

I magine a world without milk-shakes, ice cream, or cheese-burgers. Without symbiosis, that's the kind of world we'd have, because the mammals that produce milk can't digest the tough cellulose in the plants they eat. They need the help of microscopic partners.

Cows belong to a group of animals called ruminants (ROO-mi-nants). They

are the grazing animals that eat now and chew later. Today's cattle graze safely in fenced fields, but their ancient ancestors didn't have that kind of protection, which may be one reason why their system of eating developed. The only protection bison, deer, antelopes, and other wild ruminants have is speed and numbers. Animals that have to keep a constant watch for predators are better off if they can bolt down their food and chew it later.

As a grazing animal, a cow has no teeth on her upper jaw. She can't bite off grass and leaves. Instead, she sticks out her long tongue and gathers in a clump of grass, almost the way an elephant uses its trunk. By thrusting her jaw forward, she can tear off the grass against the teeth of her lower jaw and chew it with her big grinding molar teeth.

A cow's stomach has four pouches, or chambers. When the cow swallows the partly chewed grass, it goes into the first chamber, called the rumen, where millions of microscopic partners go to work.

Bacteria and other one-celled animals called protozoans ferment, or break down, the tough cellulose in the grass into materials the cow's stomach can absorb.

After the food has been in the rumen for a few hours, the cow brings a chunk of it back up into her mouth. This partly digested food is called cud. The cow chews her cud leisurely, and when she swallows it again, the cud goes into the second pouch, where it is digested more. Then it moves on to the next stomach pouch and on into the fourth pouch, where digestion is completed. All day long, the cow brings up cud from the rumen, chews it, and swallows it again. Digestion is a cow's major job. Each day she makes about sixty quarts of saliva just to keep her cud moist enough to chew.

The bacteria and other protozoans in the cow's stomach live about twenty hours, but new ones are constantly being produced. Many extra vitamins and protein are added to the cow's diet from digesting the dead bacteria and protozoans. Nothing is wasted. In exchange for their work, the one-celled animals get free food and housing in a safe, warm, wet, airless place. They are anaerobic (an-air-O-bic), which means they can only survive *without* oxygen.

Rabbits also need help digesting the cellulose in the plants they eat, and they, too, have bacteria partners in pouches in their intestines. At night in their burrows, rabbits eliminate pellets different from their daytime droppings. These nighttime pellets consist mostly of bacteria and partly digested food. When they nibble on the night pellets and swallow them, rabbits get extra vitamins and other nutrients.

All plant-eaters, or *herbivores* (ERB-e-vorz), rely on some kind of microscopic partners to help with digestion. But some herbivores—horses, elephants, and pigs, for example—don't chew cud because their systems work differently. Meat eaters, or *carnivores* (CARN-e-vorz), don't need microscopic partners because they don't eat plants.

Omnivores (AHM-ni-vorz) are animals that eat both plants and animals. We are omnivores, but we don't have the kind of symbiotic partners that can digest cellulose. When we eat leafy vegetables or bran and other grains, we absorb the minerals and proteins, but we eliminate the cellulose in those foods as roughage (RUFF-age). But like other mammals, we do have bacteria in our intestines that do an important job. The organism called *E. coli* (ee-CO-lye) produces vitamin K, which is necessary for the clotting of blood. Even though we get some vitamin K from cabbage and egg yolks and other foods, bacteria are the chief source of this important vitamin.

When we take antibiotics, we may get intestinal upset and diarrhea, because the medicine kills all the bacteria in our intestines. It doesn't hunt down just the bacteria that are making us sick; it also gets rid of our helpful ones. Our intes-

tines don't settle down and work well again until new colonies of these bacteria take up their chores once more.

Imagine a world where wood doesn't rot and nothing decays. Without symbiosis, that's what we would have. Although termites have jaws strong enough to cut through wood, like the cow they'd starve to death if it weren't for the masses of one-celled protozoans that digest cellulose for them. If you looked at the hindgut of a termite under a microscope, you'd see swarms of these creatures jostling and milling around.

With chemicals called enzymes, these protozoans break down the cellulose into material termites can digest. The termite's protozoans also have help from bacteria and fungi that feed on the digested wood, turning it into vitamins useful to both the termite and the colony of tiny partners. Newly hatched termites don't have any protozoans, but they soon pick them up in the crowded nest.

Although more than three hundred different kinds of protozoans are known to live in termites, each kind of termite has specific protozoan partners. Scientists can identify a termite just by knowing the kinds of protozoans it lives with.

Nobody wants termites chewing on a house, but termites do have a very important job. Long before there were people and wooden houses on earth, termites were chewing up dead trees and leaves as part of nature's essential cleanup crew.

6
PARASITE PARTNERS

Tigers, cobras, hawks, and sharks are predators. They kill quickly. In a way, the symbiotic partners called parasites are predators, too. In fact, some scientists say the only difference between predators and parasites is the time they take to kill their prey.

When a short, slimy worm called a leech sucks blood from a horse, we say it's a parasite. But if that leech sucks all the blood from a snail and kills it, the leech becomes a predator. A parasite is successful only as long as its prey stays alive. If the host dies, the parasite dies— unless it can quickly find another healthy host.

An animal parasite lives on food taken directly from another living animal. Some parasites change hosts often, but others live from birth to death in or on a single host. Among all the members of the animal kingdom, there are more parasites than free-living creatures. Almost all animals, including humans, have

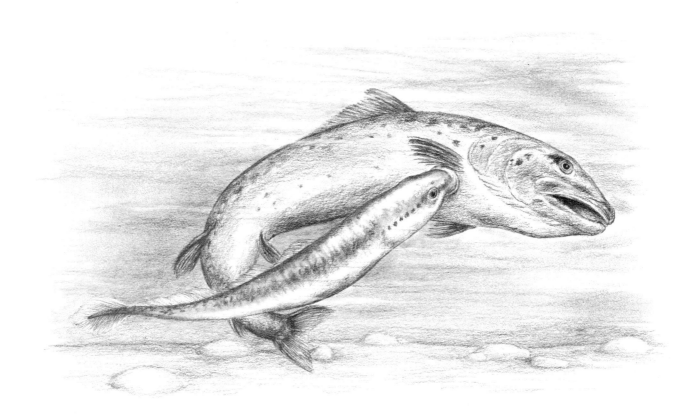

one or more kinds of parasites at some time during their lives. Even parasites have parasites! Fleas may have smaller fleas upon their backs and parasites inside them.

The sea lamprey, which looks like an eel, is related to an ancient armored fish that lived millions of years ago. It's a jawless fish, with no bones, scales, or fins like true fish. Instead of jaws, the lamprey has a mouth that is a suction disk full of scrapers. That disk is so strong that a lamprey can use it to climb right up a straight wet wall.

When a lamprey attaches itself to a fish, it scrapes a hole through the fish's skin and sucks out the blood and other tissue. Small fish are killed by such attacks. But now and then a fisherman lands a large salmon or sturgeon that wears an old scar showing where a lamprey had a meal.

Sea lampreys must move into fresh water to lay their eggs. American sea lampreys swim from the Atlantic Ocean through the St. Lawrence River into Lake Ontario. They used to stop there because they couldn't get over Niagara Falls and into the other Great Lakes. Then, in 1829, the Welland Canal was built between Lake Ontario and Lake Erie to carry freighters past Niagara Falls. When the lampreys found their way through the canal, they invaded the other Great Lakes, too. They destroyed so many lake trout, whitefish, yellow pike, and blue pike that the fishing industry and sport fishing were just about finished.

But after American and Canadian conservationists studied the life cycle of lampreys, they found a way to control these parasites. First they built electrified wire fences, called weirs, across the mouths of streams where lampreys spawned. A lot of lampreys were turned aside and trapped at the weirs, but many made it through and continued to feed on game fish. Then scientists found a combination of chemicals that killed only the larvae of young lampreys, without killing other fish. Since then, the lakes have been restocked with Chinook and coho salmon and several kinds of trout. Some sea lampreys still live there, but the fishing is good again in the Great Lakes.

There are many other parasites that live outside their hosts, like the lampreys. We may not think of fleas, lice, bedbugs, and mosquitoes as parasites, because they don't stay on a host very long. But even though they bite and fly away, they are parasites because they feed on the blood of their hosts. Except for a sting or bite, these annoying parasites may not hurt the host directly, but some of them spread terrible diseases.

One kind of flea carries a smaller parasite that inflicts the bubonic plague. In the 1300s, when the plague killed one-fourth of the people in Europe, it was called the "black death." The fleas lived on rats that swarmed everywhere—on garbage dumped in the streets and in open sewers. Today the bubonic plague can be controlled because we know how to keep our cities cleaner.

Body lice are parasites that cling to the hair and clothing of their human hosts. Like fleas, they pierce the skin and suck out blood. The bite itself isn't dangerous, but lice carry a dreadful disease called typhus.

Only the female mosquito bites, and when she does, she injects a bit of her own saliva first. That keeps the blood from clotting and the mosquito can drink her fill. If the mosquito is carrying any disease germs, they're injected into the body with the saliva. The female *Anopheles* mosquito carries a one-celled parasite that causes a disease called malaria. Another mosquito, called *Aedes*, carries a virus that causes yellow fever.

A hiker can pick up a parasite called a tick while walking through a field and not even know the tick has burrowed beneath the skin, until the tick is gorged with blood. Ticks are host to smaller parasites, including the organisms that

cause Rocky Mountain spotted fever and Lyme disease.

Unlike sea lampreys, mosquitoes, and ticks, most parasites live *inside* their hosts. Tapeworms have become such successful parasites that they do not even have mouths or digestive systems of their own. With hooks on its head, the tapeworm simply attaches itself inside the intestines of a human, a cat, a bird, or almost any kind of vertebrate, where it soaks up the already digested food.

The head of a tapeworm has not only hooks but suckers, too, for hanging onto the host. The rest of its body is built of segments that are added on as the worm grows. The newest segment is next to the head. A tapeworm may be longer than twenty feet, with thousands of segments. If we eat raw or undercooked fish, pork, or beef, it's possible to eat some tapeworm eggs that might be embedded in that meat. But we're safe from tapeworms if we eat only cooked meat and fish, because any tapeworm eggs are destroyed in the heat of cooking.

Parasites do not attack an animal because they are "bad," any more than a tiger attacks its prey because it's vicious or nasty. It's not a matter of right or wrong in the animal world. Each creature is only following its built-in plan for survival. Even though they may not help their hosts, in some cases parasites are helpful to humanity.

There are about fifty thousand different kinds of wasps that lay their eggs inside the eggs or adults of other insects, or in living caterpillars of moths and butterflies. When those parasitic wasps' eggs hatch into larvae, the larvae eat their way out of their living host. Although this may seem gruesome, the wasps are killing off some of the insects that might otherwise destroy acres of crops we need for food. Where parasitic wasps are at work, we don't need to spray chemical pesticides to get rid of some of the insects that damage farm crops and forests.

7
NATURE'S
BALANCING ACT

How did some of these partnerships get started, especially those that are a matter of life or death? How does a plover know it's safe to walk into the mouth of a crocodile? Was the first encounter between the bird and the big reptile accidental? Did many plovers get eaten because they misread a crocodile's yawn as an invitation to walk in for lunch? How did they learn the signal for teeth-cleaning time?

Or how did a clown fish first find

out it could live safely within the stinging tentacles of an anemone? And how did it pass along that good news to other clown fish?

How did a wasp discover that its eggs would hatch and find food inside a caterpillar?

Nobody knows. There are still many mysteries about the partnerships of symbiosis. But scientists believe that in the struggle for life, these animal partners happened upon some arrangement that made it more likely that they and their offspring would survive. Charles Darwin, a scientist born in 1809, used the phrase "survival of the fittest." He didn't mean that only the biggest, fiercest animals eat the smallest, weakest animals. Of course that happens. Big predators eat small prey. But Darwin was also saying that the animals that find a way to fit into a niche (pronounced "nitch") are more likely to survive. A habitat is the animal's address. A niche is the animal's role in that habitat.

More species of animals live side by side in peace than in combat. In symbiosis, animals work together in the most intense and intimate kind of cooperation between species. In one-sided commensal partnerships, in mutual-benefit partnerships, and even in parasitic partnerships, each animal has found a niche that allows its offspring to survive.

But animals can also cooperate in ways other than through symbiotic partnerships. For example, different animals in Africa can feed peacefully on the same tree. A giraffe reaches the highest branches of an acacia tree to pluck leaves from between the thorns. A long-legged, long-necked antelope called the gerenuk stands on its hind legs to nibble on the middle branches of that tree, while a rhinoceros is chewing on the lowest leaves. And smaller antelope such as the dik-dik browse on low-hanging buds, new twigs, and seedpods. These animals cooperate. Each has found its niche, but they are not symbiotic partners. They don't rely on one another. The giraffe can still eat the acacia leaves, whether the other animals are feeding there or not.

A bird called the nuthatch hunts for insects on the same tree with a bird called the brown creeper. Although they compete for the same food, they have each found a niche that allows them to get enough to eat. The brown creeper starts at the bottom of a tree and spirals upward around the trunk. When it gets to the top, it flies to another tree and begins again from the bottom up, searching for insects hidden under loose bits of bark. The nuthatch goes in the opposite direction. It is called the "upside down bird" because it walks down the tree trunk headfirst, picking up insects on top of the bark. While these birds have each found a way to get food from the same source, they are not symbiotic partners. They don't need each other, but they are part of nature's balancing act.

We hear about the "balance of nature," but nature is never truly balanced. It doesn't stand still. It's forever shifting and changing. When two species continue to compete for the same food or the same territory, the more successful one eventually forces the other out.

When starlings were imported from Europe to Central Park in New York City in 1890, they competed with bluebirds for the same food and nesting places. The starlings were certainly successful! Huge flocks of them thrive all over North America, but the bluebird is so rare that many people have never seen one.

The starling-bluebird competition was man-made. What powerful partners we are in nature's balancing act! How easy it is for us to cause unfair competition between animals, or to compete with animals for the same territory, and win. We can pollute an environment or wreck a habitat, as we did in the case of the large blue butterfly, when we broke up an animal partnership that had worked for centuries. Or we can learn that cooperation between animals and humans is possible, too.

INDEX

Anemone, 15, 17, 18, 23
Antelopes, 25, 43
Anting, 14
Ants, 11–14
Aphids, 11

Bacteria, 29, 31
    anaerobic, definition, 32
    E. coli, 32
Balance of nature, 44
Bedbugs, 38
Birds:
    bluebird, 44
    bluejay, 14
    brown creeper, 44
    cattle egret, 25
    chickadee, 28
    chipping sparrow, 28
    cowbird, 26
    honey guide, 26, 28
    nuthatch, 44
    oxpecker, 25
    plover, Egyptian, 24
    robin, 14
    slate-colored junco, 28
    starling, 44

Bison, 26
Bubonic plague (black death), 38
Buffalo, 25
Butterflies, 12
    large blue, 12, 14, 44

Carnivores, 32
Cats, 9
Caterpillars, 12, 14
Cellulose, 29, 31–32, 34
Central Park, New York City, 44
Cleaner fish, 20
Columbus, Christopher, 22
Commensal partnership, 9, 12, 22, 43
Commensalism, definition, 9–10
Coral reef, 10, 15
Cows, 10, 29–31
    cud chewing, 31
    rumen of, 31
Crocodiles, 7–8, 24–25, 41

Darwin, Charles, 43
Dogs, 9

E. coli (bacteria), 32
Elephants, 25

Enzymes, 34

Fish:
    barracuda, 20
    blenny, 20
    clown fish, 15, 17 18, 41
    damselfish, 15
    grouper, 20
    horse mackerel, 18
    manta ray, 20
    moray eel, 20
    remora, 9, 22
    sea lamprey, 37, 40
    senorita, 20
    shark, 9, 20, 22, 35
    sharksucker, 22
    wrasse, 20
Fleas, 9, 36, 38
Formic acid, 14

Gazelles, 25
Giraffes, 25, 43
Grasshoppers, 25
Great Lakes, 37

Herbivores, 32
Hermit crabs, 23
Honey badgers, 26, 28
Honeydew, 12
Hosts, 9, 36, 38, 40
    human, 36, 38, 40

Jellyfish, 18

Lake Erie, 27
Lake Ontario, 37

Leeches, 35
Lice, 38
Lyme disease, 40

Mosquitoes, 38, 40
Mutual partnership, 9, 43
Mutualism, definition, 9

Niagara Falls, 37
Niche, 43

Omnivores, 32

Parasites, 35–38, 40
Parasitic partnership, 9, 35–38, 40, 43
Parasitism, definition, 9–10
Plant lice, 11
Portuguese man-of-war, 18
Predators, 20, 25, 35–36, 43
Protozoans, 34

Rabbits, 32
Rats, 38
Rhinoceros, 43
Rocky Mountain spotted fever, 40
Ruminants, 29

Sea turtles, 22
Social symbiosis, 28
Symbiosis:
    definition, 9–10
    as cooperation, 43

Tapeworms, 9, 40
Termites, 34
Ticks, 25, 38, 40

Typhus, 38

Vitamin K, 32

Warthogs, 25

Wasps, parasitic, 40, 43
Welland Canal, 37

Zebras, 25